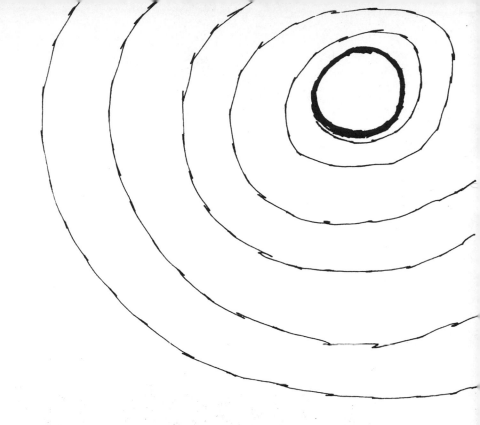

A Book of
OUTER SPACE
for You

a book of OUTER

by Franklyn M. Branley

Thomas Y. Crowell Company

SPACE for you

Illustrated by Leonard Kessler

New York

To D. F. B.

L.C. Card 71-94790   ISBN 0-690-15473-9
                            ISBN 0-690-15474-7 (LB)

4   5   6   7   8   9   10

BY THE AUTHOR

A Book of Satellites for You
A Book of Planets for You
A Book of Astronauts for You
A Book of Moon Rockets for You
A Book of the Milky Way Galaxy for You
A Book of Stars for You
A Book of Mars for You
A Book of Venus for You
A Book of Outer Space for You

The earth and the other eight planets of the solar system, the moon and the other thirty-two satellites of the planets, the sun, about 100 billion stars, and the space between the stars make up the Milky Way Galaxy. Beyond our galaxy there are other galaxies. There are billions of them. And each galaxy is made up of billions of stars. These billions of galaxies, and the space between them, make up the universe.

Some of the planets are huge—much larger than the earth. Some of them are smaller than the earth. Almost all of the stars are very big. The sun is a star; a million earths would fit into it. But the sun is only a medium-sized star. There are stars so big that a million million earths would fit inside them. All the planets, and all the stars—big as they are—make up a very small part of the universe. There is more space in the universe than anything else.

Suppose you had a huge ball, with the earth at the center and the moon going around the rim in its orbit. The ball would be about 480,000 miles across. The space inside the ball would be about 58,000 billion cubic miles. That would be the volume of the ball. The earth and the moon together take up only 260 billion cubic miles of the ball. The rest—about 57,750 billion cubic miles—is space. That's a lot of space.

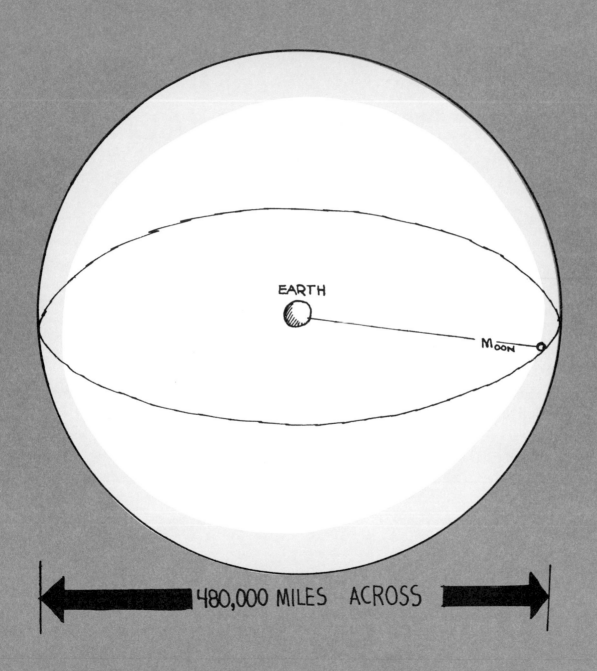

EARTH

Moon

480,000 MILES ACROSS

And that gives an idea of how much space there is in only a tiny part of the universe. Suppose you had a much larger ball—one with the sun at the center. All the planets would be inside the ball. Pluto, the outermost of all the planets, would be going around the rim of the ball.

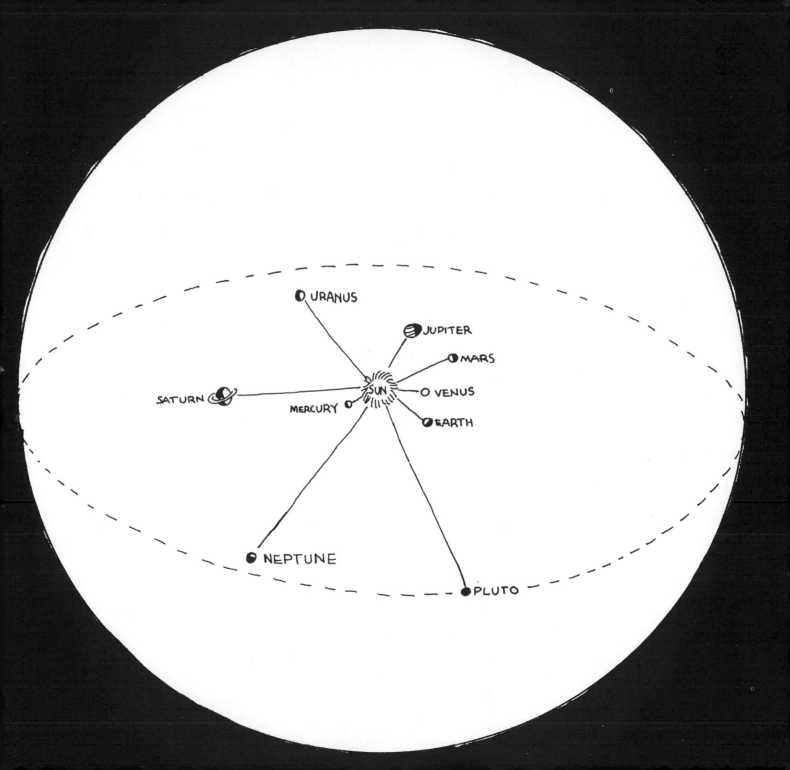

Here's how you could figure out the volume of the ball with the solar system inside it. The equation for the volume of a sphere is: Volume $= 4/3 \pi r^3$, where r is the distance from the center to the rim. The distance from Pluto to the sun is 3,600,000,000 miles. So the volume of the ball would be $4/3 \times \pi \times 3,600,000,000^3$, or $4/3 \times 3.1416 \times 3,600,000,000 \times 3,600,000,000 \times 3,600,000,000$. The space inside the ball, in cubic miles, would be more than 195 followed by 27 zeros— 195,000,000,000,000,000,000,000,000,000.

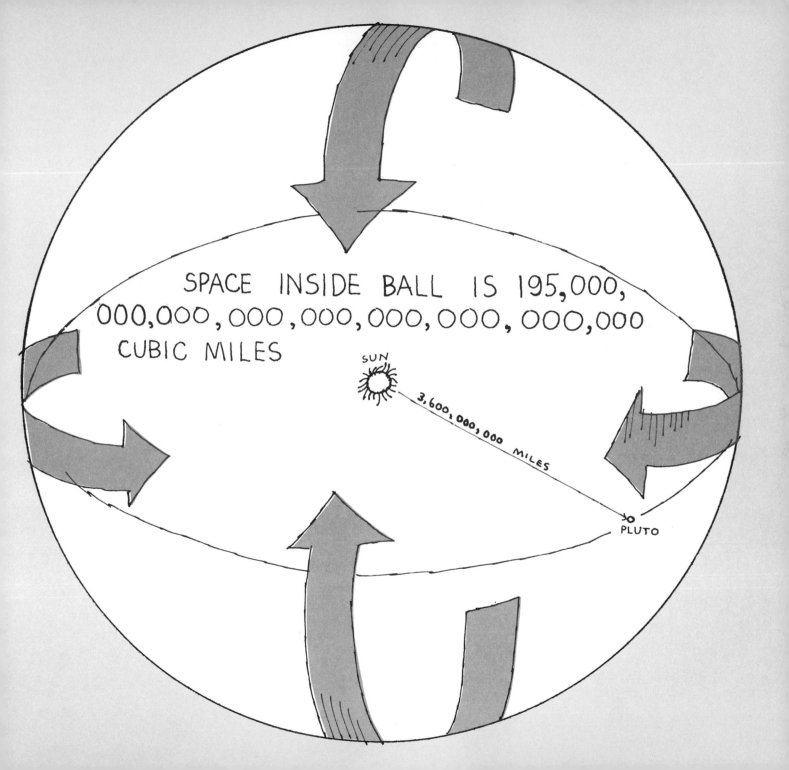

If the sun and all the planets were shown by this tiny ball, the space they occupy would be so huge that we could show only a small part of it on a whole page of this book.

There certainly is a lot of space in the solar system.

But the planets of the solar system seem very close to one another when they are compared with the stars. There is much more space between the stars than there is between the planets.

Suppose you were in a spaceship that could leave the solar system, and that you were making a journey to Alpha Centauri— the star system nearest the earth and the solar system.

If your ship traveled 100,000 miles an hour, it would take 5 years to reach Pluto, the outermost planet of the solar system. But Alpha Centauri is so far away that you would have to travel through space for 30,000 years to get there in your fast-moving spaceship.

There surely is a lot of space in our galaxy.

The space between the planets is called interplanetary space. The space between the stars is called interstellar space. And the space between the galaxies that are made of billions of stars is called intergalactic space.

Space is everywhere.

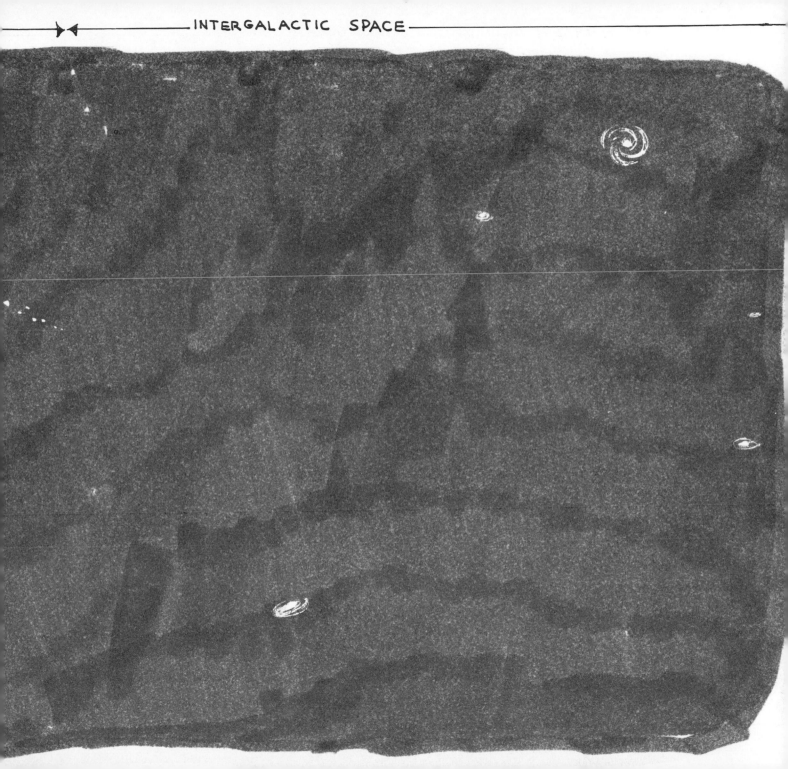

There is space between planets and stars and galaxies. There is space in the room where you are sitting. There is space between you and other people in the room.

The space in the room is not empty. It is filled with air. Swing your arms and you can feel it. Air is made of many different gases. It contains mostly nitrogen, oxygen, and carbon dioxide. The gases are made of tiny atoms or molecules. The air around the earth is called the earth's atmosphere.

Gravity holds the atmosphere close to the surface of the earth. It pulls the atoms toward the center of the earth. Near the earth's surface the atoms are packed close together. We say the atmosphere is dense. The air in the room where you are sitting has high density.

If you were on top of a high mountain and swung your arms, you would still feel the air. But you would not feel it as much as you do in your living room. The density of the air on top of the mountain is much lower than it is in the valley, because the atoms in the gases that make the air are farther apart. The farther you go from the earth, the lower the density of the atmosphere becomes.

You might think of the earth's atmosphere as a layer cake.

The layer nearest the earth, up to 1 mile or so, has the highest density. Small airplanes fly in this dense bottom layer.

The density of the air gets lower as you go into the upper layers. Jet airplanes fly in the layers 6 or 7 miles up.

Special airplanes can fly even higher, in the layers that are 18 to 20 miles up. These layers have low density. Airplanes cannot fly any higher than about 20 miles. The density of the air is too low.

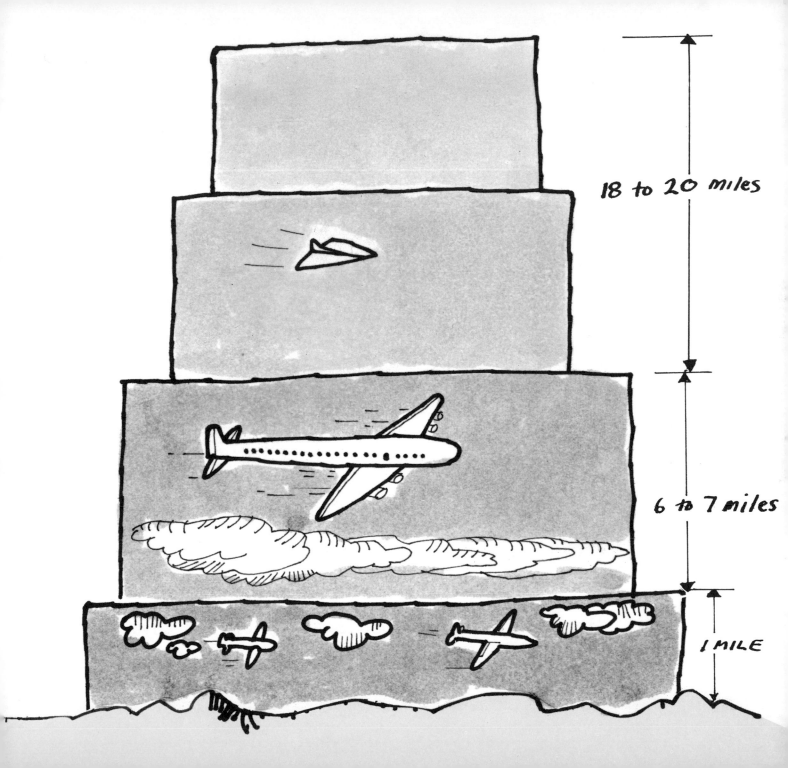

18 to 20 miles

6 to 7 miles

1 MILE

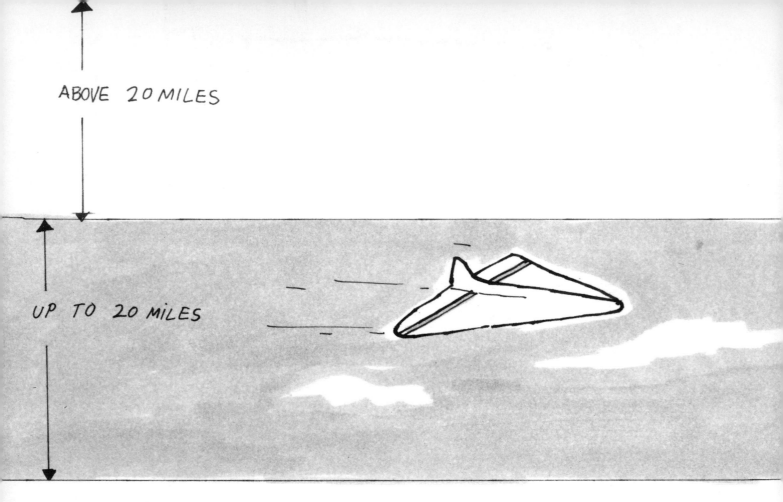

ABOVE 20 MILES

UP TO 20 MILES

Airplanes need air to fly. Their engines need oxygen. To stay up, the airplane must move through air. The air around the earth above 20 miles is not dense. There are not enough atoms to hold up airplanes.

To fly higher than airplanes can go, you need a rocket. Rockets fly best where the density of the air is lowest.

Rocket engines do not use oxygen from the atmosphere. They carry the oxygen that they need. Also, rockets have no wings. A rocket stays up because the engines push it very fast with a lot of power. The power of the engines is greater than the pull of gravity.

Rockets go so fast they cannot fly in dense atmosphere. When airplanes or

rockets travel very fast, they bump into the atoms in the space around them. This makes them get warmer. Airplanes must travel in dense air, but they do not get too hot because they travel slowly. But rockets stay up because they travel very fast. If they traveled in the dense atmosphere near the earth they would get red-hot—maybe hot enough to melt.

Two or three hundred miles above the earth where rockets fly there are very few atoms. So the rockets do not get too hot.

A rocket flies in outer space.

Spaceships fly in outer space. That's why a spaceship can go 17,000 miles an hour, and even faster, without heating up. It is in outer space, and the atoms that bombard the ship are not numerous enough to heat it up.

But even though a spaceship is in outer space, the space around the ship is not empty.

No part of outer space is empty. The space between planets is not empty. The space between stars, and between whole galaxies of stars, is not empty. Scientists believe that there is no such thing as absolutely empty space anywhere.

There are atoms in the space between the planets. There are atoms in the space between the stars, and between the galaxies. The atoms are far apart. The density is very low.

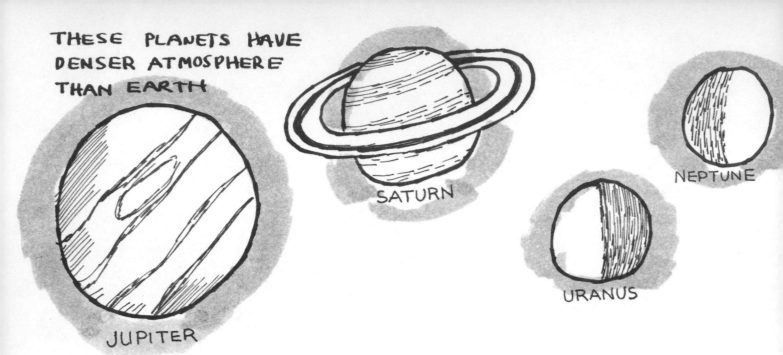

THESE PLANETS HAVE DENSER ATMOSPHERE THAN EARTH

JUPITER

SATURN

URANUS

NEPTUNE

Near the earth the atoms of the different gases are close together. Gravity holds them. There are so many atoms, and they are so dense, that we say the planet has an atmosphere.

Jupiter, Saturn, Uranus, and Neptune have stronger gravity than earth does. Each of those planets has a denser atmosphere than earth's atmosphere.

Mercury, Mars, and Pluto have weaker gravity than earth does. The atmosphere on those planets is not so dense as our atmosphere.

Venus is a puzzle. Its gravity is a little less than earth's, but its atmosphere seems to be much more dense than ours.

The gravity of the moon is less than the gravity of any planet. The moon's gravity is so low that the moon cannot hold an atmosphere.

MERCURY

MARS

PLUTO

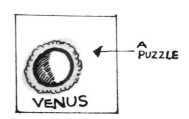
A PUZZLE
VENUS

THESE PLANETS HAVE A LESS DENSE ATMOSPHERE THAN EARTH

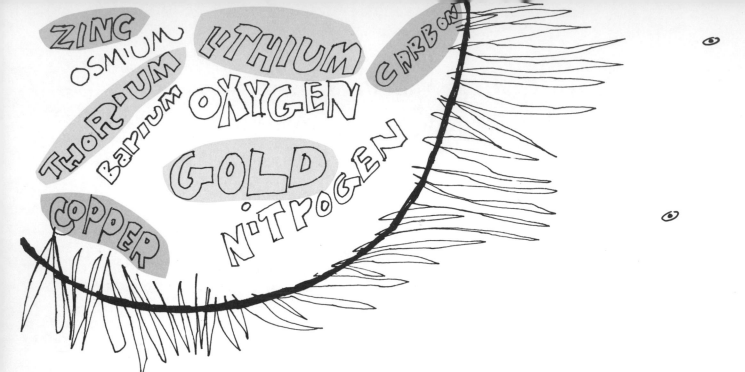

ZINC OSMIUM LITHIUM CARBON THORIUM BARIUM OXYGEN GOLD NITROGEN COPPER

In outer space—the space between the planets and between the stars—there is no atmosphere. But the space is not empty. It contains atoms of hydrogen, the lightest of all the gases. The universe is made of many different materials: oxygen, copper, iron, helium, gold, carbon. Of all the different materials, there is more hydrogen than anything else.

In the space between the earth and the sun there are billions of tons of hydrogen. In the space between the sun and other stars of our galaxy there are thousands of billions of tons of it. Hydrogen appears to be everywhere in the universe—between planets, between stars, and even between galaxies. The atoms are very far apart. The density of the hydrogen in outer space is very low.

HYDROGEN ATOMS

Men could not survive even for a few moments in outer space. We can live here on the earth's surface because it is comfortably warm—not too hot nor too cold. Also, there is just the right air pressure on the earth for man to live.

We need oxygen to stay alive. Twenty percent of the earth's atmosphere is oxygen. Oxygen is so important to man that it is often called the "life gas." In outer space there is no oxygen for man to breathe. Without this gas a man would die in a matter of minutes.

But even with oxygen a man probably couldn't live as much as a few minutes in outer space because of the lack of air pressure. Here on the earth the atmosphere pushes in on our bodies, and the air inside our bodies pushes out. There is a balance. But there is no atmosphere in outer space— so there is no pressure. In space the air inside a man's body would push outward. Since there would be no pressure pushing inward, a man would blow up like a balloon. That would be the end of him.

Even if there were oxygen to breathe, and pressure, a man could not survive in outer space because he would either freeze to death or cook to death.

A tremendous amount of heat comes to the earth from the sun. While one side of the earth is receiving heat from the sun, the other side (the night side) is losing heat. But the earth does not lose much heat at night because the atmosphere around the earth acts like a blanket. It holds the heat.

If you were in outer space, the part of you facing the sun (the day side) would get very hot. But the side of you away from the sun (the night side) would be very cold. There would be no atmosphere around you to spread the heat and to hold it in like a blanket.

Spaceships are designed to spin slowly in
outer space. That's so all sides of the spaceship can be turned toward the sun; all parts
are heated evenly.

If you were to go into deep outer space, far from the sun, the amount of heat you would receive would be cut way down. There would not be enough to keep you warm. You would freeze solid.

Man can survive in outer space only when he is inside a space capsule or a space suit. Tanks of heated oxygen keep him supplied with that vital gas. The person is surrounded by the oxygen, which allows him to breathe and at the same time keeps him from freezing to death.

Outer space is hostile to man. To survive in outer space, man must find ways to duplicate the surroundings that he is used to here on the earth.

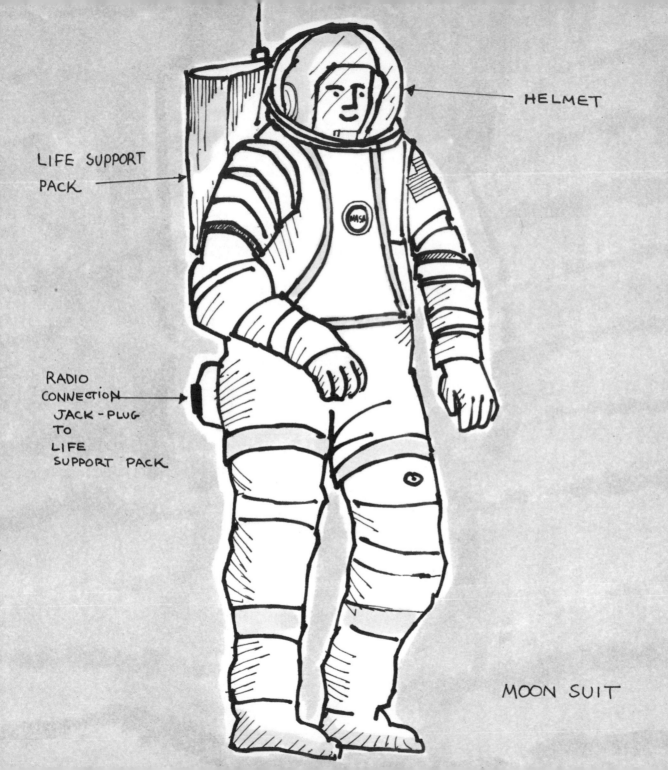

HELMET

LIFE SUPPORT
PACK

RADIO
CONNECTION
JACK - PLUG
TO
LIFE
SUPPORT PACK

MOON SUIT

On the surface of the moon, men carry air tanks and other life-support equipment on their backs. They can leave the mother ship only briefly. When men walk on the surface of Mars, they will take oxygen with them, and food and water, and equipment to keep them warm.

Man can survive in only a small part of the universe. As far as we know now, he can live permanently only on or near the surface of the earth.

Our planet is so large that men used to think it was the whole universe. But the part of the earth we see is just a tiny fraction of the whole earth. When we look out beyond the earth to the moon, planets, and stars, we still see only a tiny fraction of all there is to see. We are looking into outer space.

But what is outer space?

There is no single definition.

Some people say that outer space is any region that is not affected by planets or satellites of planets. For example, the space around the planet earth is affected by the earth. The gravitation of the earth holds the gases that make our atmosphere. It also causes atoms of hydrogen to be more concentrated in a region several hundred miles from the surface than those atoms that are still farther out.

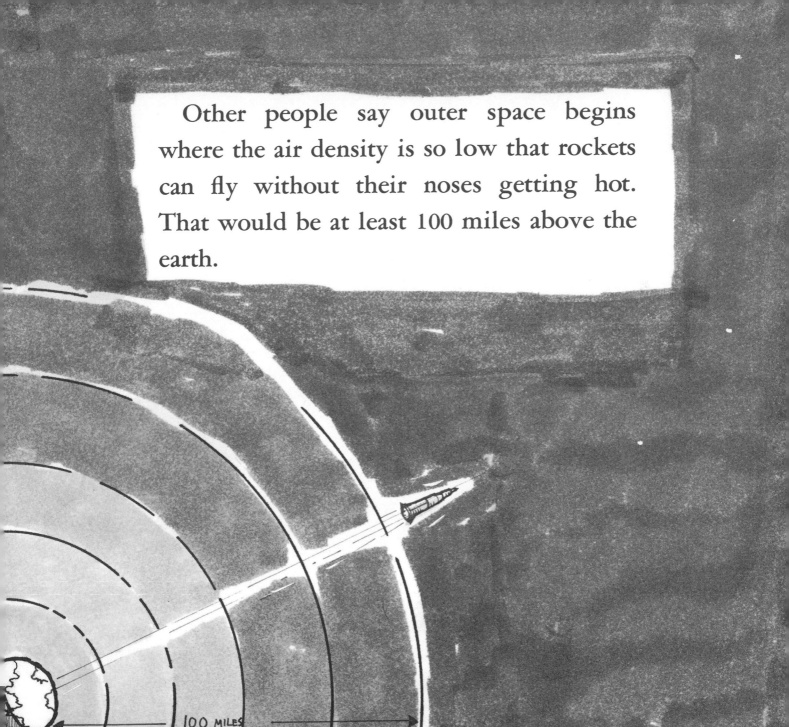

Other people say outer space begins where the air density is so low that rockets can fly without their noses getting hot. That would be at least 100 miles above the earth.

100 MILES

The region of outer space affected by the earth's presence is called terrestrial space. It's a special part of outer space.

The space around the moon is called lunar space. The gravitation of the moon is not so strong as that of the earth. But it is strong enough to pull some atoms toward the lunar surface. The density of the atoms is very low, so you could not say that the moon has an atmosphere. But the density of the particles near the moon is greater than the density of those far from the surface. The space around the moon that is affected by the moon is lunar space. Lunar space is also a special region of outer space.

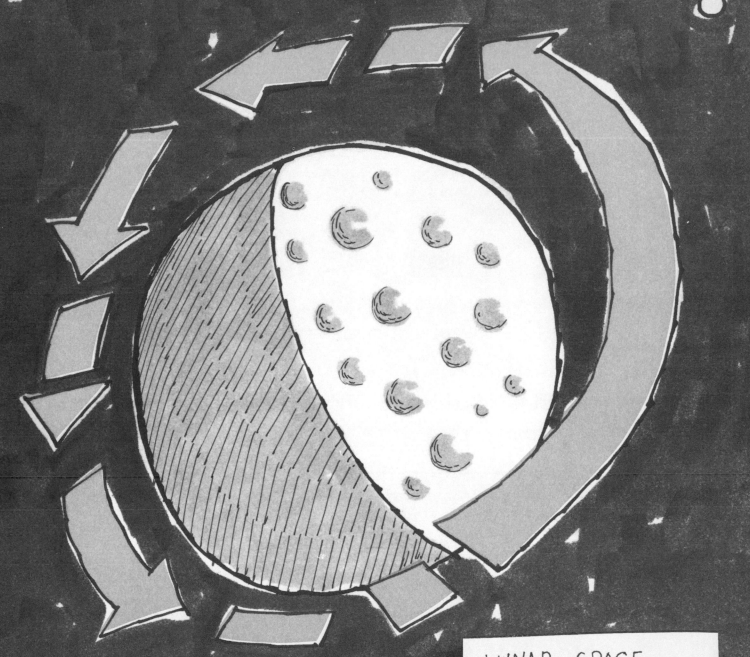

LUNAR SPACE

Still another special region is inter-planetary space. It's the area affected by the presence of the planets and the sun. For example, millions of tons of tiny bits of matter are held in this region by the gravitation of the sun and planets. Every day 2,000 tons of this material falls on the earth. Also, billions of particles, smaller than atoms, are ejected from the sun and stream through this region. They travel from the

sun to and past the planets at speeds measured in millions of miles an hour.

So far men have explored firsthand only terrestrial space and lunar space. The beginnings of explorations of the space around Mars and Venus have also been made. Someday man will set his sights on other worlds: Jupiter, Saturn, even Pluto. Men will travel deep into the cold, desolate emptiness of interplanetary space.

Outer space offers endless new frontiers. As we learn to make long space voyages, men will cross those frontiers. They will journey into interstellar space—the space between the stars. And someday generation after generation of human beings will spend their lives aboard a ship that will travel through space that seems to have no end; they will journey forever in the absolute isolation of the space between the galaxies.

ABOUT THE AUTHOR

Dr. Franklyn M. Branley is well known as the author of many excellent science books for young people of all ages. He is also co-editor of the Let's-Read-and-Find-Out Science Books.

Dr. Branley is Astronomer and Chairman of The American Museum-Hayden Planetarium in New York City.

He holds degrees from New York University, Columbia University, and the State University of New York College at New Paltz. He lives with his family in Woodcliff Lake, New Jersey.

ABOUT THE ILLUSTRATOR

Leonard Kessler is a writer and illustrator of children's books as well as a designer and painter.

Mr. Kessler was born in Akron, Ohio, but he moved east to Pittsburgh at an early age. He was graduated from the Carnegie Institute of Technology with a degree in fine arts, painting, and design. Mr. Kessler enjoys playing the clarinet in his leisure time. He lives in New City, New York.